Would You Believe...

a circus horse could count?

and other extraordinary entertainments

Richard Platt

OXFORD
UNIVERSITY PRESS

Contents

OXFORD
UNIVERSITY PRESS

Great Clarendon Street, Oxford OX2 6DP

Oxford University Press is a department of the University of Oxford. It furthers the University's objective of excellence in research, scholarship, and education by publishing worldwide in

Oxford   New York

Auckland   Cape Town   Dar es Salaam
Hong Kong   Karachi   Kuala Lumpur   Madrid
Melbourne   Mexico City   Nairobi   New Delhi
Shanghai   Taipei   Toronto

With offices in

Argentina   Austria   Brazil   Chile
Czech Republic   France   Greece   Guatemala
Hungary   Italy   Japan   Poland   Portugal
Singapore   South Korea   Switzerland   Thailand
Turkey   Ukraine   Vietnam

Oxford is a registered trade mark of Oxford University Press in the UK and in certain other countries

British Library Cataloguing in Publication Data

Data available

ISBN: 978-0-19-911871-7

1 3 5 7 9 10 8 6 4 2

Originated by Oxford University Press

Created by BOOKWORK Ltd

Printed in China by Imago

WARNING: *The practices in this book are for information only and should not be tried at home!*

Introduction

I T'S A PERSONAL THING, entertainment. Me, I like the movies. Other people prefer to listen to musicians beating out rhythms on drums made of cheese, or watch someone swallowing molten lead, or cheer warriors as they fight to the death in a bloody arena.

All these things are entertainment – or used to be. People will queue or push to watch every spectacle you could imagine and many more that you could not. Entertainment can be exciting, extraordinary, dull and even disgusting. Would you pay to hear a man farting the national anthem? Hmm, I thought that might be your answer!

You can learn all about these ways of amusing yourself in the pages that follow, but don't be tempted to stage your own performance. Some entertainments from the past, such as bear baiting, are cruel or illegal. Others demand great courage, a lifetime of training and a reckless attitude to safety! Now read on and discover that there are entertainments much wilder and weirder than anything you'll see on TV.

Would You Believe . . . ?

What, who, when and how?
What piece of music was completely silent? What is the trick to swallowing a sword? Who crossed Niagara Falls on a tightrope? When did entertainment begin? How did fools amuse kings? If you want the answers, turn the page.

Ancient
Entertainments

Prehistoric rock paintings at Newspaper Rock, Utah, USA ▶

WHAT DID STONE AGE PEOPLE DO for entertainment on long nights in cold caves, when TV was 20,000 years in the future? We'll never really know, because fun and laughter do not leave a record in the soil the way pots, bones and stone tools do. But we can guess.

Some early people daubed pictures on their walls, giving an indication of what they enjoyed. If you are imaginative, you might guess they show a party. But anthropologists (scientists who study these things) suggest that the figures are dancing up good luck for a hunt.

Hunting party ▲
From at least 20,000 years ago, people painted busy figures on cave walls. The paintings, and movements that they show, perhaps aim to give hunters magic control over their prey. Were these hunting dances the origin of the waltz and the jive?

▼ **Bull leaping**
Over 4,000 years ago, young men and women on the Greek island of Crete vaulted over charging bulls. A spectacular entertainment for those watching, bull leaping was part of the religion of the Minoan people, who worshipped the bulls.

Oldest instruments ▲
A bone with the marrow sucked out makes a tube that's easily turned into a flute – perhaps the oldest musical instrument. This flute player was painted 2,500 years ago on an Etruscan tomb in Italy.

Killer guitar
Ancient archers may have been extremely enthusiastic musicians. A bowstring will hum or twang musically when rubbed with an arrow or plucked. Bending the bow tunes the note and fixing a hollow gourd to it makes the sound louder – creating a Stone Age guitar or violin.

Singing to protect against evil may seem superstitious, but sports crowds still cheer on their teams with "lucky" songs

A few people living in the world's most remote places still perform songs, dances, plays and rituals for good luck. To them, dancing is more than entertainment. It wards off evil and makes crops grow. Indeed, it is essential to life itself.

● ● ● ● ● ● ● ●

Goroka Mudman ▶
Covered in mud and wearing masks, people who live along the Asaro river in Papua New Guinea dance with their weapons. This tradition honours the local river god who they believe saved their ancestors in battle by covering the warriors in grey mud. Mistaking them for ghosts, their foes fled.

5

CHOCOLAT GUÉRIN - BOUTRON

ROMAINS - GLADIATEUR

LES COSTUMES - (1ᵉ SÉRIE.) - ANTIQUITÉ & MOYEN ÂGE 13

BEASTLY, BLOODY and barbaric, Roman "games" were actually deadly battles. While up to 50,000 people watched in a specially built stadium, gladiators (warrior slaves) hacked at each other with weapons or braved the teeth of ferocious wild animals. These shows began in 264 BCE as religious ceremonies in which three pairs of gladiators fought to mourn the dead after a funeral. They proved so popular that politicians began to stage them to win support and votes.

Gladiator battles grew enormously in popularity. In 107 CE, 10,000 gladiators fought. The sport ended only when most Romans had become Christians and had lost their taste for such a bloody entertainment.

▲ **Proud warrior**
Most gladiators were prisoners of war, slaves or criminals. Usually only men fought, but Emperor Nero forced even women and children into the arena. Trained in special schools, the best gladiators became famous and wealthy, and were able to retire. Far more died in the arena.

Would You Believe . . . ? Would You Believe . . . ? Would You Believe . . . ?

Lion legend
When the slave Androculus faced a lion in the arena, it licked his face! Years before, while he'd been on the run from his master, he had made friends with the same beast, after pulling a thorn from its paw. Because of the moving story, Emperor Tiberius decided to free both of them.

Golden victory ▼
This gold coin shows Nero rewarding a victorious gladiator with a laurel crown. Winners in combat also got money. One retired gladiator was tempted back into the ring with an appearance fee of 20 kg (44 lbs) of gold – worth £175,000 (US $350,000) today.

Charioteer ▲
Gladiator battles were not the only Roman games. Chariot races were also popular. Drivers like this man whipped a team of four horses round the 1,200-m (1,310-yd)-long Circus Maximus racetrack that you can still see in Rome. Up to half a million people watched.

Animal combat ▼
In the 2000 movie *Gladiator*, tigers surround the hero Maximus (Russell Crowe). The reality was crueller. Tigers and other wild beasts were so frightened that handlers had to drive them into the ring with fire, to die on gladiators' swords.

Glass helmet ▲
This bottle is shaped like the helmets of secutors, gladiators whose foes wielded three-pointed tridents. To keep out the sharp tips, secutors wore helmets with tiny eye-holes.

Praising the Gods

◀ **Pharaoh's drama**
Drama began 4,500 years ago in ancient Egypt. An annual play at Abydos, a sacred place, celebrated the death and rebirth of Osiris, the god of life, death and fertility.

THE THROBBING beat of music and the physical rhythm of dance send out powerful messages of faith. Pagan priests used movement and song in religious ceremonies long before the start of Christianity and Islam and the world's other great religions. In seasonal folk festivals that continue to this day, you can still trace the ancient links between entertainment and worship.

The links are there in Christianity, too. Once learned and loved, Christmas carols are never forgotten. And the sheer beauty of religious music and drama means that even atheists (non-believers) can enjoy a Mass, a requiem or a Passion play.

● ● ● ● ● ● ● ● ● ●

◀ **Mummers**
In some European countries, masked performers called mummers visit households in traditional, annual ceremonies watched by big crowds. This Bulgarian Kukeri mummer dances to wild drum and pipe music to celebrate winter's end.

◀ **Aztec dancing**
In ancient Mexico, people sang and danced in circles to the music of drums. Many dances were religious, in honour of the country's gods. But the people also danced for fun.

Pagan rituals

It was in pagan religions that entertainment and worship merged most completely. In Aztec festivals, singing and dancing were essential parts of ceremonies in which priests cut out beating human hearts!

◀ ● ● ● ● ● ● ●

Would You Believe . . . ?

Passion play
Every ten years, the German town of Oberammergau performs a seven-hour-long Passion (Easter) play. Around 2,000 of the town's 5,000 people take part in the performance. The show began in 1632 as a way to thank God for protecting the town from a deadly plague.

Spanish monks banned Aztec love dances full of "wriggling and indecent mimicry ... a dance of immoral men"

◀ **Papantla flyers**
In a sacred Mexican dance, *voladores* (flyers) from the country's Papantla region circle a towering tree trunk above an amazed audience watching beneath. The dance honours the Aztec god Quetzalcoatl, and was ancient even when Spanish warriors discovered and conquered the country 500 years ago.

9

Music or just Noise?

Termite tube ▲
The didgeridoo is an instrument made by insects. Termites hollow out the tree branches on which Native Australians blow their low notes.

Mexican maraca

YOU CAN MAKE MUSIC with just about anything that gets the air vibrating, because music, like all sound, is just a rapid stretching and squeezing of the atmosphere. What makes musical notes different from a throbbing noise is their tunefulness – the evenly spaced steps in pitch from bass boom to high squeak. Musicians learned how to create these magic intervals about 35,000 years ago.

Even tiny cymbals can be tuned to play a definite note. ▶

◀ **Sugar skeleton**
This jolly skeleton is a sugar offering made for Mexico's Day of the Dead festival. Although he's playing a harmonica, he could be making music without it. Human skulls have been turned into rattles and drums, and ancient Tibetan flute players made instruments from human leg bones.

Ancient musicians discovered that if they shortened tightly stretched strings by different amounts, they could create higher notes. Armed with this powerful knowledge, they went on to create instruments from wood, metal, gourds, dog skins, cat guts – even cheese!

You're ribbing me! ▲
This rattle from the Spanish island of Lanzarote makes music from sheep long after their last "baaa"! There is a long tradition of making music from dead beasts. Bones make a noise when you strike them, and our meat-eating ancestors had plenty to choose from after a hunt.

Gamelan music ▲
Musicians from different cultures do not always share views on what sounds good. For example, gamelan orchestras from Indonesia, shown here on an ancient carving, play notes rising in uneven steps. To Europeans who like the evenly spaced notes from a guitar, the best gamelan can sound clanging and tuneless.

▲ **1812 Overture**
Russian composer Piotr Tchaikovsky included cannon fire in his *1812 Overture*. To avoid injuries to the orchestra and audience, cannonballs are not loaded when the piece is performed today.

Aeolian harps need no player. Gusts of wind blowing across their stretched strings coax out haunting melodies.

Musical Madness

THE CONCERT HAS begun, but the musicians sit still and silent in front of their instruments. After a few minutes, the conductor bows and the audience applauds. This silent piece, called *4'33"* (*Four Minutes and 33 Seconds*) was written by composer John Cage in 1952. Is it music or just madness? It challenges ideas about what music ought to be, and it's worth remembering that what's ordinary today caused outrage in the past.

Russian composer Igor Stravinsky's ballet *The Rite of Spring* might have been better named The Riot of Spring. At its first performance in Paris in 1913, the audience booed, argued, fought and then caused a riot. Today, audiences applaud when it is performed.

Revolutionary music ▲
Daniel Auber's opera *The Mute Girl of Portici* stirred up listeners when it was performed in Brussels in 1830. The audience rioted, starting a revolution that led to Belgians rejecting Dutch rule and forming their own country.

◄ **The Rite of Spring**
Like the music, the costumes for this ballet now seem attractive, but the first audience hated the performance. They were annoyed by the discordant notes and unusual dances.

Audio tutu

Just like *The Rite of Spring*, serious modern music aims to be challenging, absurd, exciting and above all new. It may not be popular today, but in the future, who knows? Even *4'33"* is not just wasted time. It makes the audience listen to slight rustles and noises they don't usually notice. And if music is supposed to be soothing, what could be more soothing than silence?

John Cage's work *As Slow As Possible* **is now being played in the German town Halberstadt. It will last 639 years!**

13

Tragedy, History
or Comedy?

WOULD YOU GO TO THE THEATRE if half the cast were drunk, the other half were naked and some of the audience were sacrificed at the interval? This is what productions were like when drama began in Greece 2,600 years ago, as part of the worship of the god Dionysus.

Masks ▲
Early Greek actors covered their faces with masks to show even those far from the stage what sort of characters they were playing. Comedy/tragedy masks have become a standard sign for theatre.

Most early Greek plays were histories, but the themes of comedy and tragedy quickly developed. With satire (witty attacks on human weakness), these became the main themes for all European plays.

◀ **Shakespearean theatre**
Although comedies such as *A Midsummer Night's Dream* (left) are among the most popular works of 16th- to 17th-century playwright William Shakespeare, he also wrote histories and tragedies.

The colour of the flag over Shakespeare's Globe theatre in 16th-century London showed whether the day's play was a tragedy, history or comedy.

◄ **Thai drama**
Masked pantomimes are just one of several forms of traditional drama in Thailand. As narrators describe what is happening, actors in luscious golden costumes and crazy hats act out the drama.

Kabuki actor ▶
Japanese Kabuki theatre began in Kyoto around 1600 and is still popular today. Actors whiten their faces and use grease-paint to show characters. For example, villains wear blue or black lines.

Eastern theatre

As in Europe, theatre in Asia grew out of ritual and worship. Hindu legends record that the god Brahma taught wise man Bharata Muni about drama around 300 BCE. Later on, trade, religion and conquest spread shared themes such as puppets, music and dance between countries.

15

Banning Enjoyment

Would You Believe . . . ?

Banning Christmas
English Puritans banned the celebration of the Christmas and Easter festivals, passing laws that made even eating a crime. Soldiers patrolled the streets of London, sniffing the air for the smell of roast goose and seizing the food when they trapped law-breakers.

WHAT DO MUSIC, FILMS, plays, dancing, flying kites and racing pigeons have in common? All these entertainments have been banned in the past as dangerous, "sinful" or wrong. As early as the 5th century BCE, Greek thinker Plato believed plays were imitations of real life and tried to have them stopped. He failed, but more recently some religious groups have succeeded.

When strict Christians called Puritans briefly controlled Britain and America in the 17th century, they stopped anything "ungodly". That included theatre, dancing in couples and church organ music.

▲ **Sex and violence on screen**
Should love and hate appear on television? Most TV stations can show kissing and cuddling, but no more while children are watching. There are fewer limits on hate. By age 18, most children have watched 40,000 TV murders.

Banning the bear ▲ ▶
British Puritans hated cockfighting and bear baiting. They didn't care that these spectacles were cruel, but disapproved of audiences betting, drinking and swearing. To stop the sports, they killed the bears and chickens.

Immorality

The kill-joy Puritan attitude to entertainment was deeply unpopular, and the bans didn't last long. However, controls on what people could see, hear or do for pleasure continued. The rules aimed to keep enjoyment "moral" – good, right and not harmful to those who took part.

◄ Following Hays
The Hays code made sure bedroom scenes could not shock by insisting that the cast all kept one foot on the floor. Even before the code began, sex hardly featured in films. In *It Happened One Night* (1934), a blanket screen separates the unmarried couple. Prudish audiences still complained about nudity.

Portraits ► were banned by the Taliban, except on passports.

Setting the standard
Deciding what's moral isn't easy. Rules change with time, and every country has its own standards. Afghanistan once had some of the strictest laws (see below), but in the Netherlands almost anything goes. Most other countries restrict how sex and sometimes violence can appear on screen and in print.

The Taliban ►
If Delawar (right) had flown his kite over his home town in Afghanistan between 1996 and 2001, he could have gone to jail. The country's Muslim rulers, the Taliban, outlawed kites – along with music, dancing, shaving, pigeon racing and all pictures of human faces.

A Taliban official suggested that if people wanted entertainment they could go to the park to see the flowers

17

Performers or Prisoners?

Animal welfare groups believe that it's cruel to train circus elephants. ▶

Insect entertainers ▼
Hair-thin gold wires keep the cast of a flea circus from escaping. Hitched to a cart, this one can pull hundreds of times its own weight. A man as strong for his size could drag a railway train loaded with passengers.

ANIMALS THAT PRANCE, count or read are astonishing, but is it fair to make beasts do tricks to amuse us? Nobody cared 3,200 years ago, when a trained lion called Antam-Nekht performed for Egyptian pharaoh Rameses II. Then – and for centuries after – people believed animals were created to benefit people. "Savage beasts" deserved to perform because the human was a better, smarter species.

The aim of animal trainers has usually been to make their performers as much like people as possible. In 1758, the Amazing Learned Pig filled London theatres by pointing at a circle of cards to spell simple words. Who would bother to queue to see a pig do piggy things?

Banking on dog tricks ▶
Dogs can be trained to do many things. Jumping through a hoop, as shown on this coin bank, is a simple task. One dog starred in an 1861 opera, *Barkouf*, written by Jacques Offenbach!

◀ Snake charmer
Popular in India, "charmed" snakes rise naturally from a basket when the lid is lifted to let in light. They sway to follow the movements of the pipe played by the charmer, who keeps just out of striking range.

Old-fashioned animal acts were often cruel. Trainers sometimes beat their pupils if they made a mistake. For wild animals like lions, just living in a cage was a form of torment.

A swarm of trained bees covered the face of showman Daniel Wildman while he stood on the saddle of a horse

Circus animals today

Modern animal acts rarely use wild beasts. The performers are domestic or farm animals, and trainers rely on rewards, not punishments. Circus supporters argue that training a dog to do elaborate tricks is no different from making it beg for a biscuit at home.

Gifted gammon ▶
Though not the only educated porker, the Amazing Learned Pig was certainly the best known. He beat humans to the top of the bill at London's Sadler's Wells theatre, before touring the country. Some people said he should be in Parliament.

Smart nag ▶
Horses that told fortunes or had other amazing skills were especially popular in the 17th and 18th centuries. In reality, the horses were obeying their masters' signals, which were too subtle for the audience to spot.

Fools and Jesters

Commedia dell'Arte ▼
Colourfully costumed and masked, the harlequin figure on this poster began as a jester character in the 16th-century Italian *Commedia dell'Arte* (play of professional artists).

I N THE CIRCUS TENT, clowns try to make us scream with laughter, but they once had more important jobs. From the Romans on, emperors and kings employed them because only a clown dared to tell a ruler that he was wrong. Also known as fools, jokers and jesters, these royal clowns mocked the mighty and the powerful. Their jokes were rude, but the advice they gave was often very wise and useful to a ruler.

◄ **Claus Narr**
German jester Claus Narr let out the castle bears by mistake. He knew he would be punished by having his ears cut off, so he told his dog not to tell anyone it was him – but so loudly that everyone heard!

Kings chose outsiders as jesters. Now we'd say these people were disabled or had learning difficulties. Then they were called "dwarfs", or "simple". They were often like sons to their masters. England's Henry VIII gave jester Will Somers costly clothes and had him painted into royal portraits.

◀ Tarot fool
Turned over by a fortune-teller, the fool card from a tarot pack means "passionate, insecure, extravagant". As the joker, it is also found in packs of regular playing cards.

Pantomime ▶
Crude and bawdy, pantomime gags poke fun at authority just as jesters always did. English people copied panto from the *Commedia dell'Arte* in the 16th century.

THE CHRISTMAS PANTOMIME

European jesters used theatres instead of palaces as their stage in the 17th century, and have amused us ever since in circus and panto. There are similar clowning traditions all over the world. Today, stand-up comics still use jesters' humour to make us laugh at truths we'd usually rather forget.

◀ Native American clowns
Jokes and tricks by clowns sometimes played a special and sacred part in the religion of Native American people. Traditional clowns also just made everyone laugh. They were rude about self-important people and had the freedom to make jokes about sex and other subjects that were not normally discussed publicly because it was considered impolite.

Would You Believe...?

Food for clowns
Zuni (Pueblo Native American) clowns took part in public competitions to eat the most disgusting things they could find. They bit the heads from live mice, ate the corners of blankets or pieces of wood, then snacked on dog turds and drank bowls of urine.

Traditional doll of a Hopi spirit in the form of a clown

Crazy Feet

Ballet ▲
Formal performance dance started as entertainment at weddings. It developed in Italy, Russia and France – most steps have French names.

WHEN A NEW DANCE swept the world, newspapers cried, "Evil, indecent, foreign dance"! It wasn't a modern dirty dance causing the fuss, but the waltz, in 1816. This is now ultra-respectable in ballrooms. Partner dances began in the Middle Ages, and by the 15th century, wealthy people were taking lessons. Poor people enjoyed dances they could learn just by watching and taking part.

Modern dances like street dance are easy to learn by watching and through practice. These popular dance forms continue to develop alongside the music that accompanies them.

● ● ● ● ● ●

◄ **Fred and Ginger**
Fred Astaire's slick routines with gorgeous partner Ginger Rogers, shown here together in the film *The Barkleys of Broadway*, made him the most popular Hollywood dancer of the 1930s.

22

Street dance ▼
Spinning and popping to hip-hop or funk, street dancers challenge gravity. Since they began in 1970s USA, street styles have endlessly evolved with an energy that studio dance imitators never quite match.

Ballroom dancing ▲
Once seen as a dance for the dull, ballroom has been made more popular by the cult movie *Strictly Ballroom* and by TV competitions that expose the rivalry between duelling couples.

Would You Believe . . . ? Would You Believe . . . ? Would You Believe

Tiny toes
When ballet dancers dance *en pointe* (on tiptoe) their weight is concentrated on to a tiny area of their feet. The pressure on their toes can reach ten times the pressure exerted by the foot of an adult Asian elephant. As a result, dancers often suffer from bruised and deformed feet.

World dance
Recorded music, film and TV spread American dance everywhere, but dances rarely travel the other way. Indian Bollywood movies made Bhangra music popular in Europe, but few Asian or African dances spread far beyond their own continents.

Fred Astaire wanted perfection and once filmed a dance number 47 times before he was satisfied

Ceremonial dancing ▲
Ancient dances keep alive traditions and revive unwritten history that might otherwise be forgotten. Here, Dogon people in Mali honour their ancestors in a *Dama* memorial ceremony.

Living in a box ▼
Going to a grand opera like *The Extravagant Confusion* by Rossini (below), was a social occasion in Italy. The wealthy almost lived in private boxes. They talked, drank or played chess during shows. Some boxes had bedrooms, and shutters to block out the distracting music.

O PERA MIXES SONG, drama and orchestral music in a way you either love or hate. Fans swoon and cry over the tunes and voices and ogle the lavish sets and costumes. Other people moan about costly tickets and badly behaved divas (female opera stars), but they still hum along when they hear a famous aria (song from an opera for one or two singers).

Invented in Italy in around 1700, opera spread across Europe. Each country developed a national style. The seriousness of Italian opera led composers to write more natural or comic operas, such as Mozart's *The Marriage of Figaro*, which was first performed in 1786.

Would You Believe . . . ?

Ouch!
Women were forbidden to sing in 17th- and 18th-century music, so high parts were sung by *castrati*. These men could hit the top notes because, as boys, they had had a medical operation (castration) which stopped their voices breaking – but also stopped them from having children.

Light, junk or beggars?

Opera's winning combination of music and spectacle made it very adaptable. Popular opera has the glitz appeal of a musical. Modern shows have exciting music and funny or shocking librettos (words), and show that there's much more to opera than warbling fat ladies.

◀ Peking opera
In 1949, communists in China ordered the Peking Opera Company to use only themes of revolution. The heroes of *The Legend of Red Lantern* are workers and resistance fighters.

German composer Richard Wagner's *Ring Cycle* **can be an ordeal for audience and singers – it lasts for 15 hours**

The Beggar's Opera ▲
In his 1728 *The Beggar's Opera*, John Gay poked fun at politicians and wealthy people's interest in Italian opera. The shocking theme that the rich were no better than the poor made Gay's show extremely popular.

Junk opera ▶
Billed as "junk opera", *Shockheaded Peter* brings to life a 19th-century German book that aimed to terrify children into being good, with stories of death and disaster. Incorporating puppetry and bits of pantomime, the opera follows the traditions of comic opera and the *Commedia dell'Arte* (see page 20).

Puppet Theatre

Wayang golek puppets ▶
Most Asian puppets are worked from below. Puppeteers hold up the heads of these Indonesian *wayang golek* with a rod and move the hands with more rods. A gamelan (see page 11) plays while the puppets perform history and myth stories.

I N MOST THEATRE COMPANIES, THE CAST would complain if they were paid nothing, were made to sleep in boxes and had to die on stage night after night. This is understandable, but for puppets, these conditions are all part of the job. They can play roles that are impossible for humans, and speak lines no actor would dare to repeat.

Would You Believe...?

Puppet rivals
Traditionally, Vietnamese water puppet groups, or guilds, were fierce rivals. The all-male puppeteers sealed loyalty oaths by drinking blood. Members of a group were forbidden to marry women from other villages in case they revealed the secrets of their puppets' mechanisms.

Shadowy figures worked by rods ▲
Cut-outs like this figure from Java perform puppet shadow plays. They are usually made of paper, leather or metal foil, but puppeteers have cast shadows of melting ice, or burned paper to reveal a different metal figure beneath.

Puppets can teach audiences how to avoid catching AIDS and can spread messages of revolution. But most often, they entertain us, just as the first puppets did in Egypt and Pakistan some 4,000 years ago.

Puppets on ponds ▶
Traditional puppet shows in northern Vietnam take place on water. Puppeteers stand thigh-deep in pools to operate the wooden figures using rods, wires and strings. Monsters squirt water or breathe fire. The water keeps the controls secret.

The puppets of the French *Royal de Luxe* company are as big as houses

Pulling the strings

Early puppets were moved with simple rods or strings. Modern puppets have several people operating them. Smart movie puppets need computers and many technicians to work their actions by remote control.

Punch and Judy ▶
Puppets can make us laugh at things that are not funny at all. Punch and Judy shows, performed in a tiny cloth theatre, feature brutal violence, cruelty and child abuse.

Professor Matthew Matic ▶
puppet from *Fireball XL5*

Supermarionation ▶
1960s puppeteer Gerry Anderson made TV shows, such as *Fireball XL5*. He moved his puppets with fine wires, which also carried electrical signals to move the characters' lips. Called "supermarionation", the method was developed into more realistic "go-motion" puppetry for films like *Star Wars*.

27

Music Hall
and Variety

R AUCOUS, FAST AND OFTEN RUDE, variety shows provided cheap relief from weary lives. Variety audiences could not afford theatre or opera, where seats cost a week's wages or more. In any case, they preferred variety's mix of music, magic, jugglers, comedy and pretty girls. The mostly male audiences ate, drank and smoked in their seats, singing along with the choruses.

Variety shows began in bars, but in the second half of the 19th century they moved to theatres and became music hall in Britain, vaudeville in the USA. Variety was the most popular entertainment for working people until movies and radio lured away audiences.

Music hall ▲
By 1885, when this picture of an audience was painted, British music halls had become respectable. To attract wealthier families, the halls had banned drinking, controlled audiences and made sure that acts were suitable for women and children. Music halls survived until the 1950s, when their acts moved to TV.

◄ US vaudeville
Like music halls, vaudeville theatres kept shows clean. Comedians such as Ezra Kendall and husband and wife Joseph Hart and Carrie de Mar topped the bill, but there was a huge range of acts. Between song, dance and mime numbers, reformed criminals and budding inventors addressed the crowd.

Medicine men
Travelling acts called medicine shows sold 19th-century Americans worthless potions. Between freaks, music, magic and white-sheet ghosts, a "doctor" advertised cure-all "snake-oil". They had moved on before patients realised they had bought sugar water.

As in today's stand-up comedy, music hall comedians swapped jokes and insults with the audience

BUFFALO BILL'S WILD WEST

AND CONGRESS
OF ROUGH RIDERS OF THE WORLD.

Col. W. F. Cody
"BUFFALO BILL"
ENTENTE CORDIALE ENTRE LA FRANCE ET L'AMERIQUE

Cheap thrills

Variety wasn't the only cheap amusement in the 19th century. It was competing with the circuses, wild west shows (left) and "magic lantern" shows of projected still pictures. Variety also had to fight off moral critics who disapproved of drunkenness and saucy acts.

Wild west shows ▲

A uniquely American kind of variety, the wild west shows recreated frontier life for those too young to remember it. Cattle roping, trick riding and shooting were highlights, but shows also told stories of the west. The stories were from the settlers' point of view – Native Americans who took part played "savages" who needed to be tamed.

Burlesque ▶

In the seedier variety shows, called burlesque in the USA, long-legged dancers entertained male audiences. Burlesque performers didn't really show much of their bodies, but in the early 20th century, when these shows flourished, they were very daring. In British shows, "naked" girls were actually wearing flesh-coloured body stockings.

29

Bending
and Balancing

I F YOU THINK TOUCHING YOUR toes is easy, try licking them! For performers like this circus contortionist, it's simple. Bendy, balanced people like her start with a natural ability. Super-flexible joints help them tangle their limbs or escape from knots and locks. However, their acts would be impossible without constant practice.

Prancing, dancing and folding themselves like paperclips, agile athletes have amused kings and emperors for centuries. In the 2nd century, Roman emperor Marcus Aurelius protected high-wire artists with a law requiring a safety net.

Flexible friend ▼
Performers who contort (twist and bend) usually stretch backwards, as here, or forwards, but not both ways. Though often called "double jointed", contortionists have no more joints than the rest of us.

Would You Believe . . . ?

The art of growing
Wish you were bigger? Perhaps you could be! Clarence Willard, an early 20th-century contortionist, could stand 15 cm (6 in) taller by stretching – then shrink back to normal. Watching a parade, he terrified the crowd by stretching up to get a better view.

On the tightrope

High-wire artists balance by shifting their weight to keep it exactly above their feet. They often carry a long pole, fans or clubs, which makes it easier to balance. Expert high-wire performers practise for years, but at circus courses, children and novices can learn to walk a low rope in a day.

Famous daredevils

Who remembers the Human Hairpin, who could fold himself up? Or Del Monte, who crammed himself into a box less than 50 cm (20 in) in all directions? Most acts are quickly forgotten, but a few have become legends.

▼ **Charles Blondin**
Shown here with his tightrope, Frenchman Charles Blondin became famous in 1859 when he crossed the Niagara Falls on the USA/Canada border. He performed his high-wire act 50 m (160 ft) up.

Blondin repeated his Niagara rope walk on stilts, in a sack and carrying his manager

● ● ● ● ● ● ● ● ● ● ● ●

Frenchman Jules Léotard invented flying trapeze acts in the mid 19th century. They became the most popular circus attractions. Today, these aerial stunts still make our hearts beat faster because those who perform them risk their lives to entertain us.

◀ **Circus stunts**
Balancing acrobats like the Antalek Troupe have an ancient history and have appeared in the circus since its invention by Philip Astley in 1768. This poster is from the 1920s, when American circuses were hugely popular. They were transported around the country on special trains.

Handcuff stunts ▲
Hungarian Harry Houdini was the greatest of all escapologists. He could wriggle out of handcuffs and escape from knotted ropes. His most famous stunt, in 1912, was escaping from multiple locks while immersed in a water-filled tank.

Fire, Spikes
and Swords

TO A ROLL OF DRUMS, a performer strips to the waist and walks into a flaming oven holding raw steaks. The steaks are cooked to perfection when he steps out again minutes later. This "fire resister" was Frenchman Ivan Chabert, and he repeated his flaming ordeal many times before astonished audiences in 1818. No modern daredevil has ever tried this feat. Nevertheless, the flames, spikes and blades they endure are still seriously dangerous.

People first performed these feats to show that their religious faith protected them from injuries. Fakirs (Muslim holy men) still do this. But the spectacles are now also performed as circus stunts and in street theatre. You can even take courses in fire-walking!

Flaming shows ▲ ▶

Anyone actually breathing fire does it only once! Fire-breathers (above) really blow flammable liquid from their mouth and hold a smouldering torch in front of them to turn the jet into a roaring flame. Fire-dancing (right) fans flames into spectacular wheels. It is like baton twirling with the risk of burns. Once performed only in traditional ceremonies, fire-dancing now lights up rhythmic gymnastics and circus.

▼ Walking on nails
Deeply religious Indian fakirs walked and slept
on nails to show that God gave them the power
to endure pain. It wasn't quite as bad as it looks.
The fakirs had tough feet
from walking barefoot,
and the nails were
closely spaced to
reduce the risk of them
piercing the skin.

Indian fakir's sandals from the 19th century

◄ **Eating cutlery**
Practice is the key to swallowing swords. Performers learn to extend their neck so that their mouth, throat and stomach lie in a straight line. Then they must try not to gag, choke or swallow as they lower the sword. No tricks are involved – x-rays show that the sword goes right down!

Don't try any of these stunts at home. They could kill or seriously injure you.

33

Licensed to Thrill

Vauxhall Gardens

WITH JANGLY music, garish colours, stomach-churning rides – and often similar food, fairgrounds and amusement parks tickle all our senses. No wonder we have adored them and poured through their gates for 400 years!

Amusement parks have their roots going back to medieval fairs and pleasure gardens of the 17th century. Mechanical rides appeared 200 years ago, and were powered, at first by steam, from around 1860.

Old Soviet train in Grutas Park

▲ Pleasure gardens

Pleasure parks such as London's Vauxhall Gardens became fashionable from the mid 17th century. Some have a longer history: Denmark's Bakken (the Hill) opened as a spa water resort in 1583 and is still a popular amusement park today.

Coney Island ▶

This famous New York resort had roller coasters from 1884. Steeplechase Park opened 13 years later and increased its popularity. At the end of this race, clowns tormented riders with paddles and even electric shocks.

◀ Stalinland

Lithuania's weird Grutas Park is nicknamed "Stalinland" after Joseph Stalin, leader of the Soviet Union 1929–1953. Stalin ordered the death of millions of people, including many thousands in Lithuania. The park contains statues and other Soviet relics to remind people of a terrible period in the country's history.

se Park, Coney Island, N. Y.

442

105

Would You Believe . . . ? Would You Believe . . . ? Would You Believe

House of real horror
Until 1976, California's "Laff in the Dark" sideshow spooked visitors with a glowing body. But one day the figure's arm broke off, revealing a real human bone. Police discovered that the "model" was in fact the corpse of the bank robber Elmer McCurdy.

Visitors to Coney Island spread its fame by mailing a quarter of a million postcards every weekend

Traditional funfairs
Seasonal fairs in the 12th century, such as England's Bartholomew Fair, gradually evolved into travelling funfairs. Human or pony muscles drove the first "galloper" roundabouts in the 19th century, then steam took over. Later, electric generators made dodgems possible.

▼ Dodgems car

◄ ▲ **BonBon-Land**
Denmark's BonBon-Land wins the prize for the world's oddest amusement park. With a theme of sweets and lavatory jokes, it features vomiting rats and rides such as the "Dog-Fart Switchback", as well as these amusing rides.

▲ Roundabout

◄ Test your strength

35

All done with Mirrors

Suspended in mid-air ▼
This magician's poster from around 1935 shows levitation. The magician makes his assistant seem to float in the air, supported only by the point of a sword. Most illusions like this used a lifting device hidden by a curtain behind the conjuror.

DO YOU believe in magic? Watch a conjuror, magician or illusionist perform and you certainly will. Specially made props or well practised tricks are behind most of their acts, but not all. A few are so baffling that magic seems the only explanation.

The simplest of illusions rely on misdirection. One of the magician's hands distracts the audience while the other hides a card or produces a coin from a pocket. With practice, absolutely anyone can use misdirection to astonish their friends.

◄ The Conjuror
16th-century Dutch painter Hieronymus Bosch captured the wonder of a magician's performance in his picture *The Conjuror*. Conjurors like these were a popular attraction at country fairs all over Europe. Bosch included a little extra magic in his painting – the villain on the far left is making spectators' money disappear!

"Magic" tricks have a very long history. They may have been invented originally by gamblers, as a way for them to cheat at dice or other games, long before they were used for harmless entertainment.

Before your very eyes

Professional magic began only in the 18th century, with an act by Italian illusionist Giuseppe Pinetti. With elaborate mechanical stage props, trapdoors, escapes and mind-reading tricks, he created the craft of conjuring that modern illusionists like David Blaine still follow today.

No Western conjuror has been able to repeat the Indian rope trick or even explain how it might work

David Blaine in ice ▶
Magician David Blaine uses showmanship and endurance to bring traditional illusions up to date. In 2000, he stood in an ice block for 62 hours. The stunt was inspired by famous escapologist Harry Houdini (see page 31).

◀ **Indian rope trick**
In the world's most mysterious illusion – or hoax – Indian magicians are said to have thrown a rope into the air, where it stood up, as stiff as a broomstick. A boy assistant then climbed the rope and disappeared.

? Would You Believe . . . ?

Black magic explained
The first textbook on conjuring aimed to save witches' lives. Women who performed tricks were burned for getting help from the devil. Reginald Scott's 1584 *Discoverie of Witchcraft* showed the tricks were simple illusions and not supernatural.

Sound
and Picture

IMAGINE AN IPOD THAT PLAYS music only *you* have performed, or a cinema where just one person can watch the film. This was how sound recordings and movies began, with Thomas Edison's 1878 invention of the phonograph, a machine for recording and producing sound, and the kinetoscope 13 years later.

Gramophone ▲
Old record players, called gramophones, were powered by clockwork. They used a real needle to trace the wiggling sound-recording grooves on a disc. The horn made the sound louder.

Thomas Edison ▶
As well as cinema and recorded sound, American Thomas Edison claimed more than 1,000 other inventions. But he did not work alone. In his New Jersey laboratory, he had the help of his genius employee William Dixon, who did much of the research that led to "Edison's" kinetoscope.

Flickering peep show

The phonograph was just a toy until discs of famous musicians went on sale in 1892. The kinetoscope had more success. It was little more than a wooden box with a pair of eye-holes, yet people queued and paid 10 cents to watch a silent, flickering film lasting just a quarter of a minute!

Paintings in motion ▶
Animated films began before regular movies with actors. Emile Reynaud's "Luminous Pantomimes" projected dancing paintings on to a screen in Paris in the 1890s.

The 1894 invention of a projector created the cinemas we know today. The first films were shown in cinemas about ten years later. "Talkies" (movies with sound) appeared around 1927. The experience of watching a movie has changed little since then.

◀ **Early motion picture**
Early movies lacked sound, so they used mime artists, who were used to performing without speaking. English mime artist Charlie Chaplin became the greatest comic star of the 1920s.

? Would You Believe . . . ? Would You Believe . . . ?

Moving on
When movie projectors were invented, Thomas Edison thought they were a waste of time. He believed they would never replace the profitable kinetoscope peep shows. He told his advisers, "If we make this screen machine, it will spoil everything."

Computer-generated images ▲
Until the early 1980s, computers were not powerful enough to create moving images that audiences could believe were real. But today's machines can individually model and move each hair on a character, as on Scrat the sabre-toothed squirrel from *Ice Age: The Meltdown*.

On the Air

▲ 1950s plastic radio

1920s crystal set ▶

◀ 1930s wooden "wireless"

WHEN WARS BREAK out, celebrities divorce or your sports team wins an important match, it's hard to believe what's happened is true until you've seen it on TV. Life wasn't always like this. Until 1958, fewer than half of all families had a TV set. For the rest, home entertainment meant the "wireless receiver" (radio set).

◀ ▲ ▼ **Early radio sets**
The first radio sets were strictly for enthusiasts. Called "crystal sets", they were powered by the energy of the radio broadcast itself, captured with a long wire antenna. Listeners tuned in by tickling a crystal of a lead mineral with a thin gold "cat's whisker". Later, wirelesses were made to look more like furniture.

The first radio sets transmitted messages between individuals as Morse code – long and short buzzes. Regular radio broadcasts of speech and music began in the USA around 1920.

◀ **Education or entertainment**
This 1928 advert for a radio suggests that listeners would hear opera and other worthy, educational broadcasts. In Europe, where governments controlled stations, this was true. Radio was worthy – and dull. In the USA, shows were livelier and trashier – and much more popular!

The TV begins

Television shows began not long after radio broadcasts. Few saw them. When Britain's BBC started television broadcasts in 1929, only 30 people tuned in and 20 of them had made their own TV sets! Today, as digital television spreads to the web and to phones, it's easy to make a TV programme.

The first TV demonstration showed a picture, then played the sound

● ● ● ● ● ● ● ● ● ● ● ● ●

Sound effects ▶
Rice falling on to brown paper makes a sound very like that of heavy rain for broadcasting in a radio drama. Today, radio technicians use digital recordings of sounds as well as sound effects like falling rice to add background noise to broadcasts.

Would You Believe . . . . ?

Mad scientist
When TV inventor John Logie Baird took his idea to a newspaper office, the editor shouted for someone to "go down to reception and get rid of a lunatic who's down there. He says he's invented a seeing wireless!" In 1926, Baird gave his first demonstration of true television.

◀ **Entertainment centre**
Nothing's really new. This clunky box is the grandfather of today's "home entertainment centre". Made in the 1940s, it combined TV, radio and record player. The circular screen showed a coarsely lined picture in black-and-white. Colour broadcasts didn't begin until the 1950s, in the USA.

Public Executions

I T'S A HOLIDAY! EVERYONE GETS THE day off. Crowds block the streets, straining for a better view. Those who can afford them buy grandstand tickets. Hawkers move through the crowds selling snacks and drinks. Why? Because there's a man to be executed. It seems grisly, but until the 19th century, public executions were the most popular forms of entertainment.

▲ **Stoning**
The Old Testament and Torah (Christian and Jewish writings) called on people to execute criminals by throwing stones at them. Islamic law still permits this, though such death sentences are rare.

Citizens gathered in ancient Rome to watch criminals get nailed to crosses. In revolutionary France, at the end of the 18th century, they cheered as hated aristocrats had their heads chopped off. And in 19th-century London, people thronged the gallows to see murderers dangle from ropes.

Would You Believe . . . . ?
Death masks
French waxworks pioneer Marie Tussaud made a grim profit from the public executions in revolutionary France. She took casts from famous heads lopped off by the guillotine and used them to create lifelike wax figures for her museum in Paris, and later London.

Criminals' "last words" were often printed the day before their execution and sold at the gallows

◄ **Charles I**
After losing a civil war, England's King Charles I was publicly beheaded with an axe in January 1649. Among the watching crowd were many royalists (supporters of the king). Following the execution, the king's friends were themselves at risk, so royalists had to hide their views. This royalist finger-ring has a lid to cover the king's portrait.

Cruel and unusual

The bloodthirsty public loved executions – and so did officials, who thought the spectacles would warn others to avoid crime. Today, fortunately, public executions are seen as cruel and inhumane. They have ended even in the few countries that still punish crime with death.

On show ▶
Bodies of hanged British criminals were displayed like this to warn people who missed the execution.

La guillotine ▲
Revolutionaries in France used a beheading machine called the guillotine for public executions. King Louis XVI had his head cut off in January 1793 (above), and thousands of citizens and soldiers were there to watch.

Hang 'em high ▶
In lawless places, such as America's 19th-century frontier, crowds executed without trial those they suspected of crime. Called lynching, this gruesome public punishment needed only a rope and a convenient tree.

43

What's so Weird about That?

IT'S SOMETIMES SHOCKING HOW we amuse ourselves. In the past, cheering crowds gathered to see criminals put to death. Today, we queue to see corpses cast in plastic. But our enjoyment is not just grisly. It's weird too. Isn't silent music pretty odd?

Extraordinary amusements entertain crowds in civilised countries. We may be amazed at what people in distant times and places did for kicks, but their pleasures were hardly stranger than those of our grandparents – or our own.

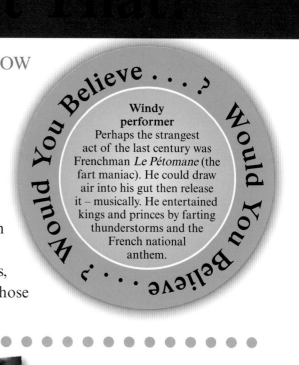

Would You Believe . . . ? Would You Believe . . . ?

Windy performer
Perhaps the strangest act of the last century was Frenchman *Le Pétomane* (the fart maniac). He could draw air into his gut then release it – musically. He entertained kings and princes by farting thunderstorms and the French national anthem.

Is it normal?

Whatever entertainment you're offered, think about it carefully before you say "Yes please." Two thousand years ago, it was considered normal to watch gladiators kill each other. Maybe in the future some of today's more unusual amusements will seem as strange as the Roman "games".

◀ **Gunther von Hagens**
This controversial German doctor entertains TV audiences by cutting up corpses. His exhibition "Body World" contains dissected bodies preserved in plastic, often standing in lifelike action poses. Critics say the dead deserve more respect.

One day people may disapprove of entertainments that use up natural resources or that harm the environment

Find out More

You can find out lots more about the history of entertainment from these websites and places to visit.

Websites

Dressed to kill
www.bbc.co.uk/history/ancient/romans/launch_gms_gladiator.shtml
Dress up your own gladiator in this BBC game to decide whether or not you survive in the arena.

All that jazz
http://pbskids.org/jazz
Join a jazz band on this website from the US Public Broadcasting Service.

Music maestro
www.nyphilkids.org/main.phtml
Compose tunes, learn about instruments, meet members of the orchestra, and more, in Kidzone of the New York Philharmonic Orchestra's website.

The Globe Theatre
http://aspirations.english.cam.ac.uk/converse/movies/sound_globe.swf
Travel back in time to when Shakespeare's Globe Theatre was the latest thing in theatre.

What a performance!
www.bbc.co.uk/northernireland/schools/4_11/sleepover/index.shtml
Find songs, scripts, costumes and scenery for a musical starring ... you!

Places to visit

Norwich Puppet Theatre
St James, Whitefriars
Norwich
Norfolk, NR3 1TN
Telephone: 01603 629921
Website: www.puppettheatre.co.uk
With live puppet performances and themed workshops there's something for everyone.

National Media Museum
Bradford
West Yorkshire BD1 1NQ
Telephone: 0870 7010200
Website: www.nationalmediamuseum.org.uk
Devoted to film, television, radio and the web, the museum is at the heart of this Yorkshire city. Entry is free but there is a charge for visiting the IMAX cinema to watch movies in staggering realism on the 14 m- (48 ft)-high screen.

Shakespeare's Globe Theatre
21 New Globe Walk
London, SE1 9DT
Telephone: 020 7401 9919
Website: www.shakespeares-globe.org
At this working reconstruction of the Globe Theatre at Bankside, on London's South Bank, you can watch a colourful performance in traditional Elizabethan costume, or see an exhibition about the original Globe and the modern building. Tickets to the exhibition also include a fascinating tour of the famous theatre.

Horniman Museum
100 London Road,
London, SE23 3PQ
Telephone: 020 8699 1872
Website: www.horniman.ac.uk
If you want to know more about musical instruments, you'll have a great time at the Horniman. The collection of more than 7,000 instruments is displayed in a gallery with videos and recordings of instruments in use. There are regular workshops with musicians.

Brighton Museum & Art Gallery
Royal Pavilion Gardens
Brighton
East Sussex BN1 1EE
Telephone: 01273 292882
Website: www.virtualmuseum.info/collections/themes/performance_gallery/html/puppets.html
The performance gallery in Brighton's wonderful museum includes Indian shadow puppets, shadow and rod puppets from Java, marionettes from Burma and Bamana animal puppets from Mali – all displayed with videos of them in action.

Glossary

Did you read anything you didn't understand?
Some of the more complicated and unusual
terms used in this book are explained here.

AIDS
Acquired Immune Deficiency
Syndrome, a medical condition
that reduces the body's ability
to fight infection.

animation
Movie-making method in which
an object or drawing is made
to move on screen by taking
repeated photographs of it and
changing its position slightly
between each one.

anthropologist
Scientist who studies the history
of human beings and what they
make and do.

Aztecs
Native Central American people
who ruled Mexico between the
14th and 16th centuries.

Bollywood
Indian musical cinema based in
Mumbai, named using the city's
previous name, Bombay, and
Hollywood, the US cinema city.

civil war
War between groups in a single
nation, not different nations.

communist
Person who believes in the fair
distribution of wealth and equal
opportunities for all.

Day of the Dead
Festival day when Mexicans
honour their dead relatives.

Etruscans
People who lived in north Italy
until the Romans conquered
them in the 1st century BCE.

gallows
Frame used for executing
(legally killing) criminals by
breaking their necks with a
knotted rope.

gamelan
Traditional musical group from
Indonesia that accompanies
dances or ceremonies.

go-motion puppetry
Animation in which models
are moved slightly during
photography to create a more
realistic, blurred motion.

Hopi
Native American people from
northeast Arizona, USA.

illusionist
Performer who tricks people in
an audience into believing they
have seen an impossible feat.

levitation
Illusion in which objects or
people seem to float in the air.

Mass
Christian ceremony in which
believers act out Christ's last
meal before his crucifixion.

mime
Silent form of drama.

Passion play
Religious drama, especially one
that acts out the last hours of
Jesus Christ, the founder and
god of the Christian religion.

pharaoh
Ancient Egyptian king, thought
by his people to be a god.

prehistoric
Taking place before written
history began.

requiem
Mass said or sung in honour of
someone who has died.

resistance fighter
Anyone who uses violence to
free their people from rule by
a political group they oppose.

revolution
Social change, often violent,
in which people seize political
power from their rulers.

shadow play
Drama in which cut-out figures
perform between a light and
a screen so that the audience
watches their shadows.

Stone Age
The time, before written history
began, when people used stone
tools and weapons.

Taliban
Military group of strict followers
of the Islamic religion who
ruled Afghanistan 1996–2001.

tarot cards
Special playing cards that
superstitious people believe
can foretell the future.

Index

Picture credits
The publisher would like to thank the following for their kind permission to reproduce their photographs:

Position key: c=centre; b=bottom; l=left; r=right; t=top

Front cover image: Lew Robertson/Getty Images

1c: Eric Isselee/iStockphoto; 4tr: Jeremy Edwards/iStockphoto; 4bl: Mimmo Jodice/Corbis; 5br: Douglas Peebles/Corbis; 6cl: Mary Evans Picture Library/Alamy; 7cr: Araldo de Luca/Corbis; 7b: Photos 12/Alamy; 8l: Image Register 256/Alamy; 9bc: iStockphoto; 9tl: The Art Archive/Biblioteca Nacional Madrid/Gianni Dagli Orti; 10cr: Karen Gentry/iStockphoto; 10tr: Martijn Mulder/iStockphoto; 10tl: Suzannah Skelton/iStockphoto; 10bl: The Art Archive.Popular Art Museum mexico City/Mireille Vautier; 11tl: Franz-Marc Frei/Corbis; 11tr: Scott Karcich/iStockphoto; 11c:Richard Platt; 12c: Lebrecht Music & Arts; 13c: Science and Society Picture Library/Science Museum; 13t: Simon Spoon/iStockphoto; 14tr: Andrew Cribb/iStockphoto; 14cl: Edward Karaa/iStockphoto; 15r: Fukuhara, Inc./Corbis; 16cr: Russel Tate/iStockphoto; 17tl: Bettmann/Corbis; 17b: James Reev/Corbis; 17cr: morgueFile; 17cr: Tomasz Pietryszek/iStockphoto; 18tr: iStockphoto; 18b: Nicole Duplaix/Corbis; 19tl: Keren Su/Corbis; 19tr: Chris Wynia/iStockphoto; 19br: Eric Isselee/iStockphoto; 20bl: Stephanie Methven/Lebrecht Music & Arts/Corbis; 20cr: Swim Inc 2, LLC/Corbis; 21c: George H. H. Huey/Corbis; 22tl: Andrew Ross/iStockphoto; 22t: Rich Harris/iStockphoto; 22cl: Topham Picturepoint/TopFoto.co.uk; 23br: Alan Tobey/iStockphoto; 23tr: Aleksey Efanov/iStockphoto; 23tl: Josef Philipp/iStockphoto; 24cl: Tristram Kenton/Lebrecht Music & Art; 25cl: iStockphoto; 25tc: Tan Kian Khoon/iStockphoto; 25r: Tristram Kenton/Lebrecht Music & Art; 26tr: Andy Green-AGMIT/iStockphoto; 26cl: Science and Society Picture Library; 27tr: Jeremy Edwards/iStockphoto; 27br: Science and Society Picture Library; 27cr: Stuart Pitkin/iStockphoto; 29br: Photofrenetic/Alamy; 29tl: Swim Inc 2, LLC/Corbis; 30b: B. Bird/zefa/Corbis; 30tr: Rosica Daskalova/iStockphoto; 31tc: Cat London/iStockphoto; 31br: Clayton Hansen/iStockphoto; 31cr: iStockphoto; 31l: Swim Inc, 2 LLC/Corbis; 32tr: Olena Druzhynina/iStockphoto; 32cl: Robert Simon/iStockphoto; 32br: Rosica Daskalova/iStockphoto; 33bl: Chris Johnson/iStockphoto; 33t: Science and Society Picture Library; 34b: Christian Klein/Alamy; 35bl: BonBonLand; 35br: iStockphoto; 35cr: James Steidl/iStockphoto; 35cr: Stephen Rees/iStockphoto; 35tl: Trolly Dodger/Corbis; 36r: Swim Inc 2, LLC/Corbis; 37bl: Levent Abdurrahman Cagin/iStockphoto; 37cr: Mitchell Gerber/Corbis; 38tc: Artem Efimov/iStockphoto; 38cl: Denie Roup/iStockphoto; 38tr: iStockphoto; 38br: Swim Inc 2,LCC/Corbis; 39b: Blue Sky Studios/Twentieth Century Fox/Bereau L.A. Collection/Corbis; 39tl: Michael Nicholson/Corbis; 40tr: Bart Broek/iStockphoto; 40tc: Gino Santa Maria/iStockphoto; 40cr: H. Armstrong Roberts/Corbis; 40tl: Ian Poole/iStockphoto; 40bl: The Art Archive; 41tr: NMeM Daily Herald Archive/Science and Society Picture Library; 41bl: Stephen Moriss/iStockphoto; 42tr: iStockphoto; 42bc: The Trustees of the British Museum; 43r: Heritage Image Partnership; 44bl: Mark Thomas/Science Photo Library

Every effort has been made to trace the copyright holders of images. The publishers apologise for any omissions.